MW00640427

IRONMAN MINDSET FOR ENTREPRENEURS

IRONMAN MINDSET FOR ENTREPRENEURS

By Robert Clinkenbeard

THE **RADIX** GROUP

Copyright © 2019 – by Robert Clinkenbeard

All rights reserved. This book is protected by the copyright laws of the United States of America. No part of this publication may be reproduced, stored in a retrieval system, or transmitted in any form or by any means, electronic or mechanical, including photocopying, recording, scanning, or otherwise, except as permitted under Section 107 or 108 of the 1967 United States Copyright Act, without the prior written permission of the author. Requests to the author for permission to use should be addressed to robert@theradixgroupllc.com

Mention of specific companies, organizations or authorities in this book does not imply endorsement by the author or publisher, nor does mention of specific companies, organizations, or authorities imply that they endorse this book, its author, or the publisher. All trademarks are the property of their respective companies. Internet addresses and telephone numbers given in this book were accurate at the time it went to press.

Limit of Liability/Disclaimer of Warranty: While the author has used his best efforts in preparing this book, he makes no representations or warranties with respect to the accuracy or completeness of the contents of this book and specifically disclaims any implied warranties of merchantability or fitness for a particular purpose. No warranty may be created or extended by sales representatives or written sales materials. The advice and strategies contained herein may not be suitable for your situation. You should consult with a professional where appropriate. The author shall not be liable for any loss of profit or any other commercial damages, including but not limited to special, incidental, consequential, or other damages. Author's results and author's clients' results are not typical, and author is not suggesting or implying reader will duplicate these results. Most people who buy any "how to" information get little to no results, especially when they aren't willing to consistently follow the suggested strategies and work hard. All successful businesses incur risks and require persistence and action. If reader is not willing to accept this, please do not purchase this book.

For general information about our products or services, please visit our website or contact:

Robert Clinkenbeard | Owner – The Radix Group LLC
CEO / Global Business Coach
Mobile/Office: 480-251-2366
robert@theradixgroupllc.com
www.theradixgroupllc.com

Publihers Cataloging-in-Publication Data
Clinkenbeard, Robert.
Ironman Mindset for Entrepreneurs.; by Robert Clinkenbeard
xxx pages cm.
ISBN: 978-1-7335648-0-9 paperback
           978-1-7335648-1-6 ePUB
           978-1-7335648-2-3 Mobi

Printed in the United States of America

Dedication

To my Dad: Thank you for the inspiration to write this first of many books. Your dedication to writing, teaching and being a solid pillar in the community has been life shaping for me and very inspirational for thousands of others around the world.

Preface

Writing a book has been on my bucket list for the last 8 years and finally everything has aligned to make this happen. Through countless hours of research, interviews with Dennis McIntee, and lots of editing, I feel excited about this first book of many. If readers obtain one or two nuggets of information from my book which will improve their business or their personal life then I feel as though it has been a worthwhile effort.

Table of Contents

"Never, never, never give up"

—Winston Churchill

Acknowledgments

To my Mum- Janette, brother- John and sister-Helen: Thank you for all you support during all my exploits and thanks for the "no drama culture" and for the all-round inspiration through our family hard work ethic, passion for travel, attitude and respect.

To my family: Thank you for just being wonderful. My amazing wife Faith and my kids Cooper, Alyx, Jack, Hunter and Harrison have been tremendously patient with my travel schedule and very supportive of my hard work ethic. Hopefully some of my entrepreneurial spirit will rub off in some way in their future.

To my EO Tribe (especially my Forum and my EMP class mates): Being around you has improved my business, my relationship with my family and has made me a better person. Being around entrepreneurs and thought leaders has been an inspiration to me and I am eternally grateful.

To my Triathlon Tribe: Your passion for competition, fitness, endurance and general translation into being good people has been very inspiring and will continue to be an energy source.

Other thought leaders and general sources of inspiration for various reasons include Dennis McIntee, Verne Harnish, Shannon Byrne Susko, Jeff Hoffman, Cameron Herold, Bruce Wilson, Keith Cupp and, finally, Joe Polish who got me very excited to make the switch to this different entrepreneurial journey immediately after our initial meeting at his office.

To everyone else who I have had the pleasure of meeting through my long journey you have undoubtably influenced my life in one form or another. I am grateful!

Introduction

This book is one of my ways in which to share some of my recent experiences in business and within my sporting passions to friends, family, my EO Tribe and fellow entrepreneurs. The goal is that with this small investment of money through the book purchase and the time reading the book the reader will receive exponential payback in one or several of the following ways:

A higher valuation of the business they are involved in.

A higher multiple when the business eventually goes through an exit.

A few more years living a healthy life surrounded by family.

Some extra time spent with the family on vacation, at sporting events etc.

The passion and excitement to still go to your office on a regular basis.

To enjoy observing the buzz and "fans" surrounding your company culture.

The thrill of experiencing the development and journey around key employees moving into senior leadership positions.

Getting extreme gratitude watching families flourish through receiving benefits and rewards from a highly disciplined, well-oiled and profitable company.

Chapter 1

Lessons in Ironman

In May of 1999, I arrived in Phoenix, Arizona with three suitcases, one newly formed friend, and the goal of creating a new and improved life in the USA. At that time, all I knew was that I had the will and determination to be successful in business and in my personal life while having the comfort of a supportive family back in Scotland. Shortly after finding my feet and breaking through some of the unanticipated barriers such as having no credit history and being new to the country, I became inspired to start a business or rise to the top in an existing business. Today, I am grateful to be healthy, to live in a beautiful part of the country with a fantastic wife and five kids in a beautiful house, and to have few financial worries. I believe that my success is due to my ability to take risks, to accept nothing less than success, and to be able change directions and adapt during times of adversity.

It was back in 2001 when my partner and I started the business. It was a humble start to the company: waking up a 3:30am to get operations kicked off in a poorly lit 8 × 5 storage unit. The long, labor-intensive days would often finish with networking and entertaining potential clients before starting the same routine the following day. I would never have imagined where we ended up taking the company's overall revenue, number of employees, and our net profit. Our success was due to some luck, a good partnership at the beginning, and the ideas that I share throughout this book. We could tell we were onto something big as we began to gain confidence and momentum, and responded to the growth plateaus by putting the systems, discipline, and people in place. In spite of having an average education and little or no money behind us, the success resulting from our passion, discipline, and will to succeed convinced me that others too can achieve a similar journey.

With regard to business, I have learned a lot over the years. Often, true learning comes from making mistakes and having the fortitude to press forward in spite of them, until one achieves success. We have all made some bad business decisions. I for one know that mine have undeniably propelled me toward even greater success than I thought possible. I've also had a lot of great experiences with both my business and my sporting endeavors: seeing great results with things that I didn't think were achievable at the beginning.

I hope, by sharing such experiences—and especially the lessons learned in the process—

that you will be inspired and filled with vision to achieve bigger and better things. Whether for your business, your marriage, your investments, your hobbies, or any other areas that require discipline, focus, and fortitude, we can all be better and see greater success!

Ironman Mindset

This chapter is about developing what I call an "Ironman Mindset" in business. Anyone who leads or owns a business knows that success is not simply measured by the bottom line. While it is easy to get caught up in the money side of business, to truly see success—long-term, sustained success—you need more than the ability to make money. You need mental toughness. Mine was significantly developed through competing in the Ironman four times. The Ironman race begins with a 2.4-mile swim, which sounds tough enough by itself. Add to it that you start the swim with 2,400 other competitors, and it is like being in a washing machine with arms and legs flailing all over the place, punches flying, and often goggles being knocked off. Many Ironman races occur in the sea, so you are also dealing with waves and choppy water. Once you get out of the water and recover from consuming excess water and exercising horizontally for an hour and a half, then you try to pull off your wetsuit and squeeze your wet body into cycling gear for a

112-mile bicycle race. During this phase of the Ironman, the challenges range from mechanical issues, headwinds, working through all the other competitors or cars, and keeping your nutrition levels high. As if that is not enough, you then finish off with a marathon when you are completely exhausted, often dehydrated, and you now experience a change in weather or temperatures. Some professionals finish the race in less than nine hours; most average competitors will finish between 11 and 16 hours. Either way, it's a brutal experience! My first one was in 2009. I was 41 years old and looking for a way to prove myself physically. When I began that first training, I did not realize how intensely I would need to train and prove myself mentally as well as physically.

Vision

When I began training for my first Ironman, I found that I could barely swim and hadn't been biking or running any significant distance before. You may wonder how I got started with such a lack of experience. The answer is simple. Early on in my training, I started to visualize myself crossing that finish line and going through all the different stages in my mind of what success would look like. My family and other supporters would be there, cheering me along. I'd cross the finish line and hold my kids in my arms. Without this vision, I would not have been able to stick with my training or complete the race. The vision propelled me forward whenever I felt like quitting.

So it goes in business. You begin with very little in the way of experience. Perhaps you have a skillset, but the depth and breadth of experience and the resulting business intuition just isn't there for you. What keeps you going at the beginning, with all the difficulties and lack of experience? Vision—seeing the end from the beginning. It is essential to crossing that finish line, whatever your business goal may be.

Unless you have that vision, you're just going to set your standards low. In the case of the Ironman, I would likely have given up. Demotivation would have set in. Vision allows you to dig deep when you experience external or internal conflict that tempts you to give up or to compromise the goals you're aiming for.

When I was training for the Ironman, I often felt like giving up, at least once a month. However, with the vision, the signs surrounding me, the people encouraging me, my skills coaches, I felt as thought I had a whole support team. I continued to picture crossing that finish line with my kids in my arms and I'd realize that failure was not an option for me. Vision does that for us—eliminates in our minds the temptation to give up.

Why is it important for business leaders to have vision? Business leaders deal with problem-solving and negativity constantly. Whether it is employee issues, client issues, cash flow issues, it seems people—ranging from your spouse, your employees, your business partner, and your clients—are constantly beating up on you. It's very easy—sometimes too easy—to be consumed by that. Perhaps there are family issues at home—maybe they're complaining about how little time you spend at home. Regardless of the issues, leaders can easily feel tempted to treat their businesses as less of a priority. CEOs or company owners can also get so caught in the daily grind that they lose sight of their motivation and direction.

Game Plan

Because of all the endless issues leaders must face, they must develop a game plan if they want to stay on track with their vision. When I trained for the Ironman, I developed a game plan early on that would keep my training moving in the right direction. I had that constant reminder: "Okay, I need to go out tomorrow. I need to ride a hundred miles to stay on track." If I didn't have that game plan, then maybe after 30 or 40 miles, I would think, "it's too hot, I'm tired, I am just going to give up and go home." But if you have that game plan *before* you go out, you're going to have a lot more focus to try to get that 100 miles completed! You must plan ahead for your nutrition, your water supply, and your route. Without this planning, forget completing the 100! There will simply be too many obstacles for that 100 miles to seem worth it without preparing everything ahead of time and anticipating your needs. Your game plan gives a sharper focus to your vision—puts it into action!

In business, we can't just show up and work very hard and expect, all of a sudden, great things to happen. You need a game plan just as much as I did competing in the Ironman! Without it, everything will just move in the direction of the wind—the easiest direction, the path of least resistance. Whether it's billing issues, employee issues, or just the daily grind—all things, by the way, that leaders *must* deal with—you will still need to set aside time in your day or week to work on your vision and your game plan for achieving it. These are the times where you must disengage from the daily grind, get out of the weeds, and ask, "Where do I want to take the company in a year? Where do I want to take the company in three years? Where do I eventually want to take the company in 10 and 20 years?"

By having that game plan, setting aside the time to cultivate your vision, and creating messaging around your workspace to keep it in front of you, you will motivate yourself to engage the daily grind. With every step toward your vision, you'll be able to look back and say, "Okay, I've done this." It will give you confidence and fresh inspiration to see your business progressing from its current state toward a full expression of the goal you've set before yourself and others.

Bring in the Experts

In training for my Ironman, I quickly found that cultivating vision and having a general game plan would not be enough to be successful. All day long I could envision crossing that finish line and having supporters cheer me on, but I could still barely swim or ride any distance. If my game plan was to ride 100 miles that day, I still needed the proper conditioning and skill-building to be able physically to achieve that part of my plan! There was a skill gap that would have prevented me from completing the race, no matter how determined and inspired I was by my vision of success. I needed to surround myself with experts who could help me to physically and mentally prepare to compete in the Ironman. I had some training partners for the different disciplines: swimming, biking, and running. They were able to push me when I was feeling tired or maybe just wanted to take a step back. They helped my competitive spirit kick into gear and stay kicked in. From the start, they helped me formulate my game plan that translated my vision into action, conditioned my body, and built up the skillsets I needed to succeed.

When I started off my bike rides, I would go out on a Tuesday or Thursday morning, and for the first three or four months the rest of the group I rode with dropped me and left me behind. At first, I was unfit for and unfamiliar with the tactics involve in cycling. There I was, in the dark, not knowing how to get home. I struggled internally during those months. I definitely felt like giving up. However, I didn't give up; I grew stronger. And the stronger I became, the more I went out on the bike, and, because I was surrounded by all these stronger cyclists, I was eventually able to keep up and lead the group!

All my coaches—for swimming, biking, and running—looked at my technical skills, where I was making mistakes and being inefficient. They helped me save a lot of time by targeting my weak spots and strengthening them. I also had an overall triathlon coach. He would say, "Okay, this is the mileage you want to keep doing this week," or, "Maybe this week's a rest week." He really helped me develop my overall game plan on how my next year was going to break down so I could be ready to compete. If it wasn't for him, I'd have been training every single week: pushing myself, sometimes too hard. He helped me dial it back every four weeks. He'd say, "Okay, this week's going to be an easy week, we're just going to dial it back, give your body a little bit of a rest." He also helped me choose the right nutrition for my training, including what I needed to eat outside of training to keep the weight down.

Similarly, you likely won't get very far in business without the right coaches and technical experts guiding you along the way. It may be an overall strategic coach that's helping you with your vision and helping to keep you accountable. It might be peer groups. (There are so many business groups out there to choose from.) The point is to make sure that you feel as though you're not in it alone.

When business leaders desire to be an Ironman in their business, it can lead to burnout. (Just like trying to ride 100 miles without having an expert nearby telling me when it's needed to "dial back" my routine and when I needed to train "full speed ahead.") They may feel as if everything is on their shoulders. This again illustrates the importance of surrounding yourself with technical experts, those who can cheer you on, and those who can hold you accountable.

By not having trust in others and by not surrounding yourself with good people, you increase your chances of being burned out in business. Without a highly competitive, driven personality, many business leaders can simply become static in their approach to business without involving others in their leadership responsibilities. A lot of business owners still have that ego, so they don't necessarily put their hand up and say they need help. This can have tragic consequences: linking to health issues, damage to family life, and even becoming a barrier to the success and future of the business. The Ironman mindset is a dichotomy of trust and humility enough to let others into your life and involve them in the successful outcomes of your business endeavors, while personally cultivating that competitive edge, discipline, and drive to take responsibility for crossing the finish line on your own terms.

Characteristics of an Ironman

Schedule. Discipline. Breaking through pain. Fearlessness. The Ironman competitor must possess all these qualities to succeed. Trust. Accountability. Humility. The Ironman competitor must also possess all these qualities to succeed.

A major part of succeeding in my Ironman—and also in business—includes surrounding yourself with experts who will help you go through the training and skill-building you need to cross the finish line. Whether, like me, the goal is to finish an Ironman in 11 hours, or to implement a successful business plan that will grow your business to a tremendous size, *you cannot do it alone!*

In business, the same characteristics apply. I call this the "Ironman Mindset." It looks beyond the bottom line, beyond the daily grind, beyond the myriad issues that business leaders face. It looks beyond all these things and seeks help from technical experts to develop the skills and competencies needed to implement an actionable, disciplined, and inspiring game plan that drives the organization toward an overarching vision.

If you get anything from this chapter, get this. To be an Ironman in your business, you must have a vision, develop a game plan to achieve it, and bring other experts into your game plan who will help you become disciplined and push you beyond what you thought you could handle.

Chapter 2

Setting Your Course: The Big Picture Behind the Roadmap

Why a Roadmap?

Just like developing a gameplan for an Ironman race, businesses must develop a roadmap if they want to see sustained success. It's really easy for business owners and people in general to go into work every day and just get caught up in that daily grind. They're happy just pushing through every day, as if they're trying to fill a hole that will never get full—trying to get to where they want to be, but with no strategic, long-term plan in place. It just feels like a thankless journey; it's not a joyful process over time.

On the other hand, having a roadmap elevates you, your work, and your employees. It generates end-results quicker and provides everyone on the team with a shared sense of purpose. It's important to be able to show your leadership team, your other employees, and shareholders where the company is going. You need to set up that line of sight for your employees and give the company some purpose and direction. Otherwise, many employees are going to think they're just going through the motions with no end in sight. That's not very motivating!

Roadmaps generate a sense of progress much faster and overall more effectively than just going through the daily routine. Because a roadmap is designed with incremental goals, you're going to see some things checked off the list as you move forward with implementing it. Typically, you'll have 10-year goals, three-year goals, 1-year goals, and quarterly goals. So, you'll be knocking stuff off the list as you move from quarter to quarter and year to year, and everybody, together, will be able to see the company progressing in a defined direction. That's motivation in itself! (On the flip side, if you stay in the weeds of the day-to-day lists, neither you nor others will see any real progress toward prescribed goals.)

When you do not see progress, over time, you and others will become demotivated. Observable, measurable progress—or even the chance of reaching a goal—provides employees with a reason to stay within the company. With a well-designed roadmap, these progress goals can improve overall employee retention and can inspire employees to tailor their professional development goals to coincide with your long-term roadmap. Also, let's just face it, although it takes a lot of work and effort, having a roadmap for your company and for yourself is personally inspiring and motivating—well worth the effort in the short and long term!

Self-Discipline

Perhaps the greatest employee payoff of developing a roadmap for your business is that it has a ripple effect in terms of discipline. When employees can be inspired and given a sense of purpose, they will have greater self-motivation and self-discipline. The purpose you inject into the business will get you excited about getting out of bed every day. It will keep you on your toes with expectation for what each new day will hold!

The Trap

A lot of business owners get caught in the trap of money-making and the daily issues that surround and complicate the process of implementing the roadmap. Whether employee issues, cash issues, or whatever, the result is (or will be) business inertia. Would the driver of a car face the open road with a full tank of gas and friends riding along with no particular destination in mind? In that case, wouldn't the riders quickly feel lost and directionless? Businesses that have not developed and begun to implement a roadmap can start to feel—both for employees and leaders—a lot like that car meandering from one place to another on the open road.

A roadmap has the capacity to take the entire company to another level—with its employees, its productivity, its culture, and its profitability. The roadmap steers employees toward a set of measurable, achievable objectives that provide employees with a sense of purpose and—if you have the right people in the right jobs and doing the right things in those jobs—an inspiring reason to get out of bed every morning and report to work. Roadmaps pave the way for businesses to be a place of life and excitement for employees. This inspiration proves to increase retention, attract talent, and boost productivity. Most importantly, the company roadmap helps leaders and employees avoid what I call a lifestyle approach to business.

Lifestyle Business

Lifestyles businesses can exist easily without a roadmap, but they will likely not grow significantly with the times. Employees and leaders in these businesses grow complacent and satisfied with the status quo of what they are doing. The danger here is the possibility that they adjust to a static way of life within the company and begin to overlook or turn down growth and development opportunities. To avoid this, you need to bring in your vision—explained routinely through a detailed roadmap—in order to steer the organization forward into fresh, inspiring, and productive territory.

As I said, without the roadmap, the predictable happens: lack of purpose leading to demotivation. Everybody becomes stuck without something to become excited about. People intrinsically need such goals that will motivate them to stay fresh, inspired, and productive. A wise man once said, "If you are not growing, you are dying." While it's unlikely that your employees would physically die without your roadmap, they will start getting bored, leaving their jobs, and possibly negatively affecting your company's culture, perhaps through rumor mills or other types of unhelpful criticism.

In leading my company, we got caught up in and stressed out about all the day-to-day details. We forgot to consistently pull back and refresh ourselves in longer-term goals. I remember one particularly bad year we went through. Initially, we were scratching our heads, trying to figure out what went wrong. We were looking for an explanation for our failures. It was a year or two later, when I started to read about how important it is to create a roadmap, that I realized it was us—the leadership team—that hadn't steered the company in the right direction. We didn't have a roadmap in place and we were not intentional about our growth plans.

Once we began creating our roadmap and displaying it around our offices, our leadership team became instantly motivated and engaged. That began to have a trickle-down effect on all the other employees. We all began working together, understanding our work through the perspective of our roadmap. More of our employees began getting behind the plan; it was creating motivation and excitement! Everyone began to realize that there was financial benefit for them personally, or that there would be opportunities to progress up through the company ranks into jobs that might open up. The key during this phase was to communicate all of this—the roadmap and resulting incentives—all the way up and down the lines of communication throughout the company. Doing this generated significant excitement toward our shared goals.

The Underestimated Impact of Excitement

The business leader often underestimates excitement. However, most business leaders value building a positive corporate culture. They somehow seem to miss the reality that corporate culture is the product of excitement—or the lack thereof—within a company. A good culture will overcome a lot of the small issues that lifestyle business companies routinely struggle with. If people get excited—are genuinely happy about being at work—then you're less likely to get HR issues that prevent progress. People will be motivated to work harder and possibly longer. There will be fewer illnesses and sick days taken— people will want to be there and not miss out!

These are just a few examples of the benefits attending a good corporate culture, which is always the product of excitement toward a shared vision and actionable goals. This brings the conversation back to what most business leaders are focused on to begin with: making money. Of course, increased profits are the natural result of shared vision and actionable goals leading to employee and leadership excitement that frames a good corporate culture. People will know, without hesitation, what they need to be focusing their work time on, because the company goals are identical across all divisions and departments within the company. Once the vision and actionable goals are clearly and routinely communicated, employees across the company will be implementing their piece of the roadmap on a daily basis.

Begin with Your Purpose

If you don't have your purpose—why you're in the business in the first place—you will have no frame of reference to understand how to begin creating a roadmap. You cannot frame a vision with goals before you know your purpose for being in business. Why do you do what you do? Do you want to build a company that inspires its employees and their families to join you on a journey? Is it a charitable or social movement that you intend to use to impact the world for good? Do you want to dominate your market?

You need to think big—bigger than any other planning required for your roadmap—to realize your purpose in business!

In order to clarify and articulate your purpose, you need to be comfortable with asking a lot of questions, both of yourself and your leadership team. Why did I start this business? What gets me excited about this business? What motivates me to continue this business? What makes me happy when I walk into your company doors on a Monday morning? These kinds of questions probe for your purpose in business. This list is not exhaustive—there are plenty more questions to ask if you start to think it through. I suggest making a list to keep up with the many things you can ask yourself and others in clarifying your business purpose.

Data Gathering

Once you've clarified your purpose, you need to look at two additional things. First, take a look at the marketplace. What kind of competition are you up against? A SWOT (strengths, weaknesses, opportunities, threats) analysis on competition may be helpful at this stage. Money is important in both business and life, but you will do yourself a huge favor to slow the process down enough to conduct a thorough SWOT analysis, both internally (in your own company) and externally (looking at competitors). If you know the strengths and weaknesses of your competition, you can leverage both to your advantage. It is likely that there are things you will not be able—at least at first—to do better than your competition. However, it is equally likely that there are things you are currently not doing that you can do better than your competition. Knowing what these things are can provide a huge advantage in setting up your roadmap for either profitability or obtaining or retaining more clients. This is admittedly a much slower process to making money than just diving in and going to work, but it will likely achieve two long-term results for your company. First, it will set you up to become a powerhouse in your industry: a standout from the competition. Second, it will increase your chances of long-term, sustained profitability.

The Value of Feedback

Another thing to pursue in generating your roadmap is to talk to your clients. In what ways do they perceive your company to add value to them? In what ways can your company better serve and add value to them—where's the room for improvement? The market is always changing and, with it, so are clients' expectations of the services you provide to them. As such, I recommend conducting this exercise routinely, in order to stay current with your client's expectations and actual needs. Ask them directly to name the top two things that they love about what your organization does. Then, be even more bold and ask hem how you can improve on those two areas and make your services more consistent across all your clients. They will be delighted to see a company pursue them in order to find out how they can pivot to meet their needs more fully.

The same (or similar) questions you ask of your clients should also be asked of your employees. Receiving their feedback on what they love most about their jobs, the company, and other components about the business will allow you to internally survey the attitudes and ideas about what you are doing best, what can be improved, and what is generally unwanted by your employees. Employee feedback is equally vital data to have when developing a roadmap that will naturally inspire buy-in from everyone who interacts with and is influenced by your business.

On top of defining your sense of purpose for business, having all this raw data—market analysis, competition analysis, client feedback, employee feedback—allows you to come to those initial leadership team meetings fully loaded to discuss the direction and framework of your company's roadmap. While it can be time-consuming, it is worth the time spent during those leadership meetings to sift, organize, and consolidate that data—distilling it into three to five great ideas that focus on what the company will look like in

10, 15, or 20 years. This is your potential BHAG®
("Big Hairy Audacious Goal")[1]—your company's
vision, which we will discuss next.

---

1 Jim Collins, author of *Good to Great*, placed the BHAG into the center
of his Hedgehog Concept, noting that it must align with all the components of your strategy. The BHAG must also align with the purpose
of the company.

Chapter 3

How to Develop the Roadmap

Culture Coach

First, let's start at the end. We have a coherent and articulate roadmap that has been communicated on every level of your organization (and continues to be). While there are different ways to develop a roadmap, with many tools and guides out there to choose from, the most successful roadmap initiative I've experienced involved having a culture coach in place that helped hold me accountable to the roadmap. This kind of coach typically has the tools, processes, and experience in place to be of great value to you. This is not so much about developing your roadmap, but how to keep yourself on track once you've developed it. If you have the absolute best roadmap in the world but lack the discipline to consistently implement it, it won't be helpful to you in business. So, the culture coach steps in and helps you keep everything on track: making sure your implementation of the roadmap remains aligned with your mission, vision, and values.

Developing a great culture—and cultivating it with the help of your culture coach—will ultimately run rings around your competition. Many leaders struggle to let go, delegate, or trust others around them. By building a high culture, articulating and repeating the vision and values, and providing the roadmap, you will be on your way to success. Therefore, before you even draft your roadmap, I suggest that you begin looking at who could help you stay accountable to implementing it.

Establish Long-Term Goals First

Sit down with the owner or CEO of the company and the leadership team. Convene a one or two-day strategy meeting and cover a clear process with a defined outcome during those two days. Make sure you're separating yourself and your team for this meeting: getting offsite so that the day-to-day work isn't looming over your meeting in the other room. You might start off with your BHAG®. What's your company going to look like in 10 to 25 years? Let's all agree on that and put it down on paper. This establishes a vision for the future. Then, eventually, you'll want to break it down further, into what I call your 3HAG[2] (Three year Highly Achievable Goal): three-year goals. You'll likely need to sift out many things that are important in order to come down to just

---

2 Developed by Shannon Susko, the 3HAG is the prescriptive framework that takes the guessing out of strategy. www.shannonsusko.com

three priorities. You'll have to answer additional questions as a team. What will success look like? Are you going to be a regional player? Are you going to double in size? You'll need to establish some really specific targets for these goals—maybe related to revenue, maybe employees. You'll start setting really specific priorities from the 3HAG and going forward (and these should align with your BHAG®). This is where all those initial thoughts about your company's purpose come into play.

When you're creating the roadmap, it's vital to evaluate the market you're in and the type of products or services you want to focus on. This is part of generating your roadmap—focus on the end result.[3] You'll want to look at competitors, your most profitable lines of business, and then figure out where you want to focus your efforts. What can you do the best and make the most money from? This is all a key part of where you bring in your leadership team. Look at all the data generated within the company and sift through everything to distill each goal level: BHAG®, 3HAG, one-year, quarterly, daily.

---

3 Jim Collins referred to this as the "Profit per X" which represents the underlying economic engine of the business and provides the leaders with a single Key Performance Indicator (KPI) they can track to monitor the progress of the business. An example of this can be profit or revenue per employee.

A Word About Core Values

Another vital component in establishing your long-term vision and goals—which needs to be reviewed in your offsite planning meetings—is your company's core values. Ironman athletes need a strong core—or midsection—to provide power, stability, and control. The same is true with growth companies. Without a strong core, the organization risks instability from disengagement, loss of focus, cultural challenges, and lack of passion. Ask lots of questions, and encourage discussion among your team members. What are your company's values? Are you comfortable with them? Do you need to review and revise them? Which ones and why? Can you live and die by these values? Can you make decisions by them?

Connected to the values conversation and building your strategy, you should be aware of your team. Does this team have the capacity to take your company to the next level? Are your A, B, and C players in line with your company's core values, or not? Should I have C players? During this conversation, I suggest that you list the values and whether the team you have working for you is the right team to take the company to the next level.[4] It's also helpful to consider if you would enthusiastically re-hire your existing leadership team. Get it down on paper. If members of your

---

4 There are many tools available to help your evaluate your team.

team are not in sync with the company's core values, it is important to evaluate whether he or she is the right fit for where your roadmap is leading the company.

Establish Signpost Goals (3HAG, Yearly, Quarterly)

Before rushing out to implement your long-term goals, you will need to slow down and highlight markers or signposts so that you don't get lost along the way. Remember, 10, 15, and 20 years are all a long way off compared to the current day. If your BHAG® is all you're aiming at, you'll likely lose sight of the vision before you get there. Signposts are needed: measurable success markers that can be achieved incrementally as you progress toward the BHAG®. They should be incrementally spaced from 10 to five years, then to three years (your 3HAG, highly achievable goals). The next step is to set your number one priority and your key initiatives for the coming year. This should include some very specific and expanded financial outcomes. I've noticed many leaders make the same mistake when setting one-year goals. They'll be so excited about their BHAG® and 3HAG that their zeal leads them to create too many priorities (or "Rocks") to realistically achieve.[5] This tendency can have a negative effect

---

5 The term "Rocks" is used in business to describe quarterly goals that are practical and achievable.

on your business culture and actually demotivate your employees rather than inspire them with vision. I recommend setting no more than three to five one-year priorities within a given year. With these, you should ask, "What do things look like now? What's our market share? What's our gross margin? Our revenue? Our profitability?" These questions will help you frame those one-year goals. Next, determine your handful of key initiatives that must be completed this year to achieve your goals. Think of these initiatives as your corporate New Year's resolutions that should be reviewed annually.

Lastly, it's important to break down the annual goals into 90-day actions (less is more) that are achievable and will keep your company employees inspired and working in the right direction. I highly recommend not setting more than five quarterly goals. I've found that more than five leads to overwhelm, which works against inspiring and empowering your leaders and employees to make progress toward your incremental goals and overall vision. Three to five is an appropriate range for quarterly goals and accomplishes three things simultaneously: gives focus, prevents overwhelm, and provides clarity on how to make progress.

Quarterly goals allow short-term progress monitoring and should always be easy to connect to the 3HAG. So, what are the three to five Rocks you want to achieve next quarter? Once you've established these, establish one person who will be responsible for each Rock so nothing gets lost along the way. These goals can be further broken down into individual tasks, but there should be one person who is responsible in the company for overseeing and meeting each quarterly Rock. It is important to choose only one person for each task in order to avoid the blame-game and confusion.

Establish a Company Rhythm for Meetings

After all these goals are set, you're still not quite ready to implement! You should assume that your company employees and leaders need help being disciplined in order to meet all these goals. This comes down to the rhythm of meetings. A rhythm is always anticipated. Likewise, your meetings should become anticipated events: something your employees and leaders can rely on regularly and be excited about.

Start with the daily huddles: 10 to 15 minutes of brainstorming, announcing big wins, or discussing challenges, either with the whole company or within each department or division. In these fast-paced and upbeat huddles, you'll just talk about some of the challenges, some of the wins, or some of the things that are coming up on a daily basis. This facilitates better overall communication, both as a team and across the organization. You'll also need to establish weekly management meetings and what I call Level-10 meetings, during which you get very focused on overcoming any roadblocks to the goals you're progressing toward daily, quarterly, and annually. These meetings normally should last about an hour and a half. You will need to establish a monthly meeting for everyone, to review and refresh everyone on the priorities you've established across the goals you've set. Are they progressing on track, do we need to go into more detail, do we need to pivot or start over?

Maintaining a disciplined meeting itinerary, from the daily to monthly meetings, is an important part of achieving the goals you set across your roadmap. Include a very structured agenda that focuses on setting and discussing priorities. After each meeting, you should have a list of action items along with an owner and deadline for each. A Level-10 meeting is an important time to involve attendees; otherwise, long meetings can get boring when you're just sitting there listening to someone else talk the whole time. However, if you have a focused meeting and you're working on your priorities or Rocks along with current problems—those things preventing you from moving forward on quarterly goals—you're going to have a lot more opportunity for input and discussion from attendees. You'll get vital feedback from these meetings to take back to your leadership team. This kind of Level-10 meeting can be a super-motivating, fun, and engaging time for everyone involved—and it should be! This is a time for everyone in the company to get refreshed on the vision, redefine and reestablish priorities, and discuss roadblocks to progress on quarterly goals.

In discussing all these meetings—daily huddles, weekly meetings, monthly, quarterly, and even annual meetings—we are talking about creating rhythms across the company. This is about discipline, but on a deeper level, it is about meeting employees' expectations for thorough, ongoing, forthright communication. One of the biggest complaints from employees everywhere is the lack of communication. These meetings help with everything—setting the agenda, including a review of your critical numbers and Rocks, refreshing everyone on goals and priorities—and they especially help with meeting everyone's expectation for communication. Establishing a rhythm to these meetings helps employees know what to expect. When employees know what to expect, you'll be working like a well-oiled machine across company departments.

Again, Communication!

In the last chapter, I made the point that excitement, in part, produces the company culture. In addition, communication—or the lack thereof—also plays a direct role in creating culture. The roadmap, at its essence, is a communication tool for your company, and a powerful one at that! Without it, there will be confusion about your company's goals that move everything toward long-term vision. Normally, a lack of communication causes employees to just make up their own storylines about the company they're working for, which, unfortunately, can end up sounding like rumors. The roadmap not only establishes purpose for your organization, but it controls the company's narrative—the company's story. Without intentionally exercising control of your company's storyline, others who are not in place to lead can inadvertently take control of the story. When this happens, goals within each department become mismatched to the company's leadership and their vision for the future of the company.

Summary

At first read, this may all sound like a complicated process, but stop and think about it for a few moments. It's all designed to simplify the process of achieving short- and long-term goals that work toward a shared purpose and vision across your company, while increasing profits.

Define your purpose. Get your data. Establish goals and signposts along the way, including: 10- to 25-year BHAG®, 3HAG, one-year priorities (three to five initiatives), and quarterly actions (three to five Rocks), daily huddles, and Level-10 meetings. Work through your core values as a team so that you know how you will make decisions. Evaluate the team to make sure you have all the right people in place, categorizing them into A, B, and C players.[6] Get it all down on paper. Then, set the meeting rhythm: daily huddles, weekly meetings, monthly, quarterly, yearly rhythms. Last but not least, don't forget to bring in your culture coach to help you stay accountable to everything related to your roadmap.

All of this helps you progress forward while not getting lost along the way and involves ongoing, deep, company-wide communication and leadership alignment. Some companies really struggle, especially when they get stuck along the way, because they lack a thorough communication effort. This whole structure is designed to facilitate ongoing, deep and wide company communication: the meetings, the roadmap, the goals and priorities (document them on the walls, literally, so people don't forget them!), and the structured meetings, so that everybody's aware of and clear on the goals. Without this level of communication, you're not going to be completely safeguarded against confusion, inefficiency, and demotivation, all of which can negatively affect company culture.

With the roadmap in place, and the right people in place, and good messaging consistent

---

6 The right people in the right seats doing the right work.

with the company's narrative, you'll inevitably begin attracting talented people to your company who identify with your narrative and your roadmap. Winners attract winners. So, in terms of attracting talent, people outside your company who find themselves inspired by what you're doing and where you're going will take note of your direction and all the cool things you have in place—and they'll want to come be a part of it!

If you choose to implement these practices in your company, you will simplify your complex business approach while making short- and long-term goals achievable, and you will do it with a roadmap that will keep you on course from start to finish.

Chapter 4

Putting Great Processes in Place

Once your roadmap is established, you've created your signposts all along the way, and have established a rhythm of meetings that everybody can rely on in the organization, it is time to establish effective daily processes. In creating your roadmap, you establish goals as far-reaching as the 10 to 25-year BHAG®, all the way down to quarterly Rocks that are each owned by one person. Your meetings include the daily huddles. Processes need to be established so that your operational movement across each workday also adheres to the overall roadmap: its vision, purpose, and methods.

Processes bring greater efficiency to your workday. They help you feel that sense of daily satisfaction, from having a productive day that you can be certain is moving in the right direction: ultimately, the direction of your BHAG®, 3HAG, yearly, and quarterly goals. Otherwise, you could go out and do a job—any job—and it could look completely inefficient. With a process, you get things down on paper and you share it with everyone in your company: with your leaders and they share it within their departments. This leads to another great aspect of having processes in place: delegation. With trust, leaders are freed from the need to micro-manage things; they can delegate with the right process underlying the daily workflow. This is especially true when you have the right people in the right seats doing the right things. You'll likely need to do some training on your process and explain why the process is helpful—sometimes employees do not see these components as easily as you will. But it will be worth it! In the short- and long-term, you'll save time and money. When you create those processes and explain their rationale to your leaders and employees to the point that they will implement them, your business will demonstrate its discipline and marketability and will show that your employees are interested in what they're doing enough to have a good system in place.

While it is possible to delegate without such processes in place, you'll lose a lot of your efficiency. In order to really infuse discipline and efficiency into your company, you'll need good processes. Often, business owners won't delegate because they lack trust in their leaders and employees. They may be a high "D" on the DISC, so they like to retain control over what they're doing. They like to be decisive and have all that knowledge for themselves. Such leaders will find it more challenging—but equally important—to establish these processes.

Roadblocks to Establishing Great Processes

Even though other leaders may not be high "D's" they could be deterred from establishing great processes due to lack of time, lack of incentive (or payoff) to begin the processes, or lack of understanding of how to document the processes in an effective manner.

How To Create Great Processes

In many cases, it is useful to have a good model—someone else you can talk to and find out what worked for them. Or, shadow someone and debrief with him/her at the end of the day while taking notes on how he created the step-by-step process. It can be difficult to determine your starting and finishing point when drafting these processes. Sometimes, it can tend to flow into areas that are really unrelated to the process; then it becomes tough to figure out where the shutoff point is.

Most important, first identify the various things for which you want to establish written processes. For example, perhaps you want to establish a process for sending out an invoice for your company. What is your starting point for that? And what would be the finishing point, once the task is fully completed? Start off there; determine the starting point and the finishing point. Then, you can fill in the different touchpoints along the way, in the middle of the process. Also, create a timeline for each process. From start to finish, how long should this take? You should work on this with those who will likely be involved in each of these processes from day to day, figuring out the most efficient ways to implement and record them.

Having processes for all the daily activities that occur within your business provides a way to measure your business's daily productivity and efficiency. If you're not producing what you would hope, you can always come back to the processes you've written down and ask, "Is there a more efficient way to conduct this process or can we outsource this?" This is a great question to ask over time, given the ever-changing nature of the business world and customer expectations and the ever-evolving nature of technology. As businesses and leaders, we should always be striving to improve. You certainly wouldn't want to be caught off guard—doubling or tripling in size in a smaller timeframe than you anticipated— without already having great processes that maximize efficiency and productivity.

When your processes are established early on, you can modify them with the passage of time, the emergence of new technologies, and the growth of your company over many years. You'll have to modify and revise your processes continually. But, you need to begin being disciplined about your processes—writing them down, delegating them, and measuring their effectiveness—early and regularly! If you have the best roadmap in the world for your company (and I hope you do!)—with inspiring vision and effective rhythms to your ongoing meetings and staff development—but you have no real processes written down for regular, daily activities within your business, you're still missing a vital communication tool for ensuring efficiency, productivity, and long-term growth. Discipline yourself and your company to take the time to collaborate and write down all those processes needed for success! Remember, an undisciplined business is like an unbalanced car. Eventually, it will veer off course. You don't have to be that car!

Chapter 5

The Circle of Respect

After you've thoroughly developed your roadmap—with the various tiers involved in developing the process and writing the final outcome, and after establishing effective procedures—there is another component that drives success beyond your signposts. This is a leadership quality that I call the circle of respect. At its foundation, it has to do with recognizing that everyone in your company is a leader in their own way, even if they are not part of the C-Suite team, managers, or directors.

Businesses all contain a circle of respect. That is to say, in businesses, respect—and down the line, the execution of your roadmap—moves in a circular direction, ultimately finding its way back to where it began. This drives profits up, dissatisfaction down, and makes business partnerships and relationships across all levels enjoyable, fulfilling, and rewarding.

The Making of a Client for Life

During off-hours one evening, we received a call from a client asking us for help. Our region just experienced a major storm and there were fallen trees everywhere: lying on cars and against buildings. It looked like a war zone! Being off-hours, all our employees had gone home, our tree crews had gone home, and the particular employee who received the call from this client of ours had gotten home and was just about to step into his house and greet his family for the evening. When he took the call at the front of his house, he could immediately tell that his client was distressed and he decided, on the spot, that he needed to help him. Our client's shopping center was home to a number of major retail brands. It was approaching a holiday shopping weekend, and those retailers had grown to expect a lot of shoppers coming in and spending a lot of money at their stores around the holidays as the norm. However, with all the fallen trees, it was unsafe to try to get there; roads were blocked and there was a lot of debris everywhere. He went inside, apologized to his family that he needed to return to work, and then he went on a mission. He began to sort out what employees were available to help him and gather the available tree crews he needed, along with all the other resources he would need to visit that property for cleanup purposes. This employee went out, himself along with those he had called on, and spent nearly the next eight hours working on cleaning up our client's shopping center so that they could open for the holiday. Numerous crews came out and removed trees and storm debris from the buildings, the cars, and the parking lot, eliminating all forms of danger from the surrounding area that would prevent shoppers from visiting over the weekend. Had he not done this for our client, with a holiday weekend approaching, there would have been no way for shoppers to access our client's places of business at this shopping center. The added kicker was that this employee took the additional step of recording all the damage and clean up through taking pictures and videos in order to help the client make a successful insurance claim. Had we not responded as quickly, there would have been a major disruption over that weekend to that shopping center's retail businesses. Many would likely have seen significant decreases in their sales for that holiday season.

Not only did the shoppers get to shop, but this employee earned our company a client for life. He treated our client like a human being, knowing that his issue with the recent storm was a real one: threatening their holiday revenue. He did not treat our client like a mere client: someone with whom we do business. He treated him with a respect that transcended normal business hours. Our client was unbelievably delighted by our willingness—represented in the actions of one of our employees—to go the extra mile for him. Afterward, he kept calling our office and even sent a letter of thanks! This client of ours became recognized within his own larger property management company for doing such a great job and was given an award! He told us all this, emphasizing how proud he was to have that relationship with our company: one that would go the extra mile. Had our employee been disgruntled with his job and position in our organization, he likely would never have gone the extra mile for our client. Again, a company's culture, in tandem with the clear communication of its mission, vision, and values, creates employees who promote long-term client buy-in.

Developing the Extra-Mile-Employee

Is there a way to develop such characteristics in your employees, in which he or she will, voluntarily, go the extra mile for a client? I believe the answer is yes and the method is simple. In the case of our employee who undertook this initiative on his own, it was simple: we treated him with respect. He had worked for previous companies that did not identify with his values and work ethic. So, we treated him really well: gave him a good position, paid him well, and provided him with great incentives and benefits. Also, we treated him like a normal person rather than like a "cog" in the machine or someone working within the ranks of a hierarchy. We listened to him and consistently expressed our appreciation for the value he brought to our company. In summary, we treated him with respect, in every way we could. Our treatment of him—coupled with his own work ethic—caused him to naturally treat our clients with the same level of respect he received from our leadership. This is the circle of respect. We respect our employees. Our employees respect our clients. Our clients, in turn, respect our company back by becoming a customer for life. The circle of respect must be part of your company's culture for you to successfully implement your roadmap.

Keys to Creating and Maintaining the Circle of Respect

Communicate openly, honestly, and often. Build trusting relationships across your company: with employees and their families. Host annual family events that bring everyone together. I have seen many successful events hosted such as BBQs, carnivals, family days at the local baseball stadium, soccer tournaments, and events around professional soccer games that facilitate relationships. Really, the keys to showing respect are to build relationships and communicate with your employees regularly. In turn, they will naturally do the same with customers. No matter how technical, strategic, and high-level your business is, the human element cannot be ignored for long if you want to be successful. Humans want to know they are valued. We respect people by seeking to know them and by communicating and listening to them: relationships and communication. Of course, this cannot be the only part of an onboarding system for new employees, but it should be a part of it, and it should continue for as long as that employee works at your company.[7] Share your expectations early as to how our employees and clients should be treated and communicated with. However, just telling people what you expect over and over again is never going to be enough. It also needs to be modeled: build up that trust and respect in your employee so that he or she will naturally act and respond to your clients in the same way.

---

7 I am a firm believer in having a party or celebration for new employees rather than for employees who leave. This includes even getting a welcome gift for their partner.

Chapter 6

Having a Great Leadership Team

What kind of leaders will produce the best results for your company—the results detailed across your roadmap? In order to identify what your company really needs, you'll have to go ask what everyone—even individually—needs, including operationally. You'll also need to discover the owner's needs. Whether you survey people or ask them individually, or use some other method altogether, once you've clearly discerned your company's needs, you will want to begin to ask the first question: what kind of leaders will produce the results, according to these needs and according to your roadmap?

Finding and developing great leadership teams is also a major part of successfully implementing your roadmap, your routine processes, and the circle of respect. Additionally, such leaders take things off your plate that you won't and shouldn't need to worry about. Most often, a good leadership team possesses diverse skills, personalities, and perspectives—ones you don't necessarily have. The variety of a dynamic leadership team can, in my experience, bring great buyers as well.

More often than not companies will struggle to reach that next upturn of growth due to being too involved in the business and working down in the weeds rather than *on* the business. I think ego often gets involved, resulting in the inability to delegate or to trust in employees. In my business, I was fortunate to tap into a seam of precious talent who were smart, hardworking, and complemented the existing company culture. As these employees became more experienced, more confident, and immersed themselves in the vision, culture, and values, the company started to experience exponential growth. Once everyone was aligned with our goals and working together, we saw improved leadership, communication, and dynamic teamwork, all of which lead to reduced staff turnover, higher sales, higher profits and, most importantly, increased take-home pay.

Techniques for Assembling and Developing a Great Leadership Team

There are surely endless ways to go about finding and assembling great leaders for your company. I'll share what worked for me. As I've said, I went through the company and identified what all my needs were: both my own and the company's (individual employees and the owners). In my particular case, it came down to three primary needs: a hunger to learn new things, people skills, and efficient processes to be put into place.

Knowing these three imperatives, I went out and studied various personality assessment systems to help me identify some key traits and how they could be combined together and in tandem with certain personalities and other skill sets. Then, I initiated an advertising process, reached out to my own network, and was able to identify some potential candidates. Once I had my candidates, I put them through a series of personality tests and interviews. I was quickly able to dial in the right match between their skills, existing employees, new people to fill in the gaps, and to evaluate them against our company values. According to the circle of respect, I made sure that respect was a part of this entire process, and that the package we offered them with their employment was generous and reflected our appreciation for the value we perceived would be added to our company with their particular personality, skills, and employment history.

Some of the skills I was hoping to match in these candidates, in addition to the three needs of our company, included: the ability to problem solve, the ability to work well under stress, and good people skills in general. They needed to be able to work effectively with the employees, the clients, and also be able to make decisions based on particular situations that arose. With the right skills, background, and experience, along with the ability to problem solve and follow the processes we had established, such leaders would be able to make the right decisions.

Problem Solving

Most leaders, myself included, do not tend to like it when their leadership team presents problems to them without also offering a solution. Problem solving is about being able to embrace the problems that inevitably arise in businesses and identify viable solutions. Leaders and leadership teams regularly face negativity, problems, and struggles in the business. In reality, they're ultimately responsible for how those issues are handled, both inside the organization and across their customer base. Without strong problem-solving abilities, a business leader will likely fail to navigate the complexities of such issues with tact, practicality, and respect for others. Rather than bring me an issue without a solution, I would rather hear about a problem that is accompanied by potential solutions. It's even better if a leader would simply fix the issue and keep it in line with the vision presented and the goals agreed upon. Ideally, the leader should be able to break the issue down into a practical timetable, work at the priorities, and put a game plan in place before even coming to me. Then, he or she should communicate our efforts to clients or the other stakeholders affected. This is a much more proactive approach to problem-solving—

that I think is far more productive and effective for businesses—than when leaders simply present the problem with a "What do we do?" mindset.

To develop these expectations and foster the correct problem-solving mentality in leaders in my organization, I would give them scenarios for which problem-solving was required. I took them to job sites. I would ask them how they (each) would handle the situation. If I couldn't get them to a job site, I'd ask them questions that posed similar scenarios, while coaching them on how to handle it correctly. In some extreme cases, I would simply tell them what to do, but most of the time I preferred to coach them with problem-solving issues until they came up with the right scenario on their own. It's important to keep in mind, in the midst of all this coaching, that the leaders still know the vision of the company, the priorities for the year, and the company's values and the outcomes we are trying to achieve. These issues must be covered extensively for the new leader before effective coaching can happen. I would do this multiple times with each leader until it became obvious that they were comfortable doing it on their own.[8] Sounds like a lot of work? Absolutely—but well worth it!

---

8 The important element of this is that the leaders still know the vision of the company, the priorities for the year, the company's values, and the outcomes we are all trying to achieve.

Working Well Under Stress

The line of work we are in—the service industry—is a thankless job with lots of stress involved. There's quite a bit of pressure to get work done, often with no finish line in sight. Sometimes, it can be really easy to get bogged down with all the stressful time constraints on the work we do. Whether it's problems with jobs, employee issues, or a lack of employees to do the work, it really is vital—both in our business and in most businesses out there—to be able to handle stress and work productively in it. The best way to approach stress in work is to decide ahead of time that you will not allow yourself to get flustered about it all. It can help to imagine a "worst-case scenario" to help you dial back the stress of your current scenario. Normally, your worst-case scenario will never happen, so it's useful to imagine what that could be; it helps with feeling more grateful for the scenario you're actually in, even though it's stressful! For example, a worst-case scenario could be if someone is badly injured on the job, or perhaps there is a fatality. That's extreme pressure! So, if it's not that, the calm approach to the current situation is easier to envision and implement. It helps, once you're calm about things, to imagine the pros and cons about the stressful situation—problem solving. Figure out the best end result and work backwards from there to create a solution. Prioritize a game plan from that kind of reverse planning strategy. I do realize sometimes just being calm is extremely difficult and doesn't work well, but I think for most things it can be a place to start under stressful conditions. It's a much better place to start in dealing with stress than just becoming overwhelmed and developing a negative outlook.

People Skills

Leaders need good people skills. This is a basic reality that cannot be escaped. In business, to sustain and nurture your company culture, you as a leader must be able to recognize and attend to the needs of your employees. To be honest, the easiest way to cultivate the kind of culture you desire in your company is to keep your employees happy while implementing your roadmap. The caveat here is, if you cannot both keep your employees happy and implement your company's roadmap, you need to consider that some of those employees may not be a good fit for your company's vision and purpose. Get the right people in and the wrong people out and you will be able to do both.

There is a second aspect to having good people skills, and it is deceptively simple. Be humble, and be kind to others. We have a saying for our kids: "You leave your evil at the door." In other words, let the best of yourself shine to others. Leave all your negativity at the door and be approachable. To be a great leader—one with good people skills—you have to be humble, willing and able to listen to people and to develop those people. You can't just criticize and blame them and expect them to be okay with that. You're the leader! Remember the circle of respect. It takes humility, especially on the part of the leaders, to successfully implement the circle of respect in business organizations.

Making Good Decisions

There is a delicate balance in business between making decisions too quickly (which often results in bad outcomes) and just making a decision at all. When either of these result, people get frustrated. When leaders don't make decisions, or fail to make decisions in a timely manner over an extended period of time, the company culture starts to become negatively affected by employee frustration. The processes you've put in place can even become compromised or break down at times. It is vital that leaders have the experience and a concept of the process in place needed to make decisions based on the best thoughts, data, and options available for the particular scenario requiring a decision. This skill can be learned, but for leaders, it is needed to one degree or another before they step into leadership positions with an organization. Decisions are what move the company's vision along the roadmap on a daily, weekly, quarterly, monthly, and yearly basis.

All leaders need to be able to problem solve, work well under stress, have good people skills, and make good decisions on a routine basis. The remaining combination of skills, personalities, and characteristics of a leader need to be carefully assembled through personality testing and extensive interviewing once you've determined what kinds of skills your leaders need to posses to fill in the gaps of your own professional experience, leadership approach, demeanor, and interests.

Chapter 7

Qualities of Great Coaches

I've talked a good deal so far about coaching and how powerful it can be. I wouldn't have been ready to compete in, and finish, the Ironman races and world championships without great coaches helping me prepare, holding me accountable, and pushing me beyond what I thought I could handle. At this juncture, you may wonder what makes a great coach—how do you assemble the best coach or coaches for the unique needs that you have for your business? I think that is somewhat of a personal question; it depends on your business and your individual needs for a coach. However, there are more fundamental characteristics of great coaches regardless of the particular issues for which you require a coach. In this chapter, I will share my list of qualities of great coaches. You should use this list whenever you're thinking about bringing on an expert, particularly someone (most likely a business coach of some kind) that you will work closely with. My goal in creating the following list has been to save you the time that would be required to conduct your own research—Internet or otherwise—

to discover what to look for in a coach. These principles are based largely on my experiences with great coaches, both for business and for my Ironman training.

Top 10 Characteristics of a Great Coach

#1: A great coach will be able to help you avoid responding out of your emotions.

In their constant dealing with negative situations and problem-solving, sometimes CEOs and other business leaders will respond more from their emotions than from logic and problem-solving processes. This can be a big mistake, especially when other people—employees, clients, colleagues—are involved or affected by your response, which can be often. With tough situations, a good coach is able to help you step back, take a deep breath, and walk with you through the situation. Emotional responses end with rash decisions that carry short- or long-term consequences. For example, if you fire somebody without going through the proper protocols, it could result in legal or other financial penalties toward your business. You could also make a decision that is based more on your ego than the most reasonable course of action. Coaches can help you navigate such decisions as a third party (you, your ego, your coach) in the situation.

When we respond from our emotions, we often do not look at the long-term consequences. A good coach will help you put your responses in perspective before you make them, looking at the pros and cons of each possible course of action before advising you on the most reasonable one to pursue.

#2: A great coach will coach you without having a hidden agenda.

Some coaches who are not properly vetted in the interview process can be found later on to have a hidden, personal agenda for working with you. Almost always, the results will not be good for you personally or helpful for your business. Perhaps the coach has some long-term engagement in mind that he wants to design to make money from you. So, rather than coaching you to make decisions easily, he could lead you down a longer back road to prolong the process. The remedy to accidentally taking on this kind of coach is to ask them a lot of questions up front, during the interview process. This leads me to another point: it's never a good idea to take on a coach for yourself or your business without a thorough vetting process in place. (Later on in this chapter, I'll share my top 10 questions to ask a prospective coach during the interview process.)

#3: A great coach will help you separate personal and company interests.

Sometimes, for business leaders especially because their work is so much a part of their lives, it becomes difficult to separate their personal interests from the interests of their company. A great coach will help you identify when this is happening and help you draw a clear line between the two when integrating them could be seen as a violation of ethics. For example, perhaps a business leader is basing a decision on some of the income that's being generated from the company. If they end up pulling cash from the company—beyond their contractually agreed-upon compensation—for personal interests, the company could be in danger of becoming cash poor. There's obviously going to the perception of personal interest involved in that transaction. A good coach will help you look carefully at the ongoing fiscal health of your business; he or she will make this the priority above your personal interests unrelated to work.

#4: A great coach will provide their extensive network to you as a resource.

If you are going to take the time and money required to hire an experienced coach, you should expect some level of access to their personal business connections. Most of the time, experienced coaches have extensive networks of contacts, representing vast domains of expertise that you might be able to draw on down the line or in the immediate future for your own business. By hiring a great coach, you are surrounding yourself with the best people that are connected to them in some way. You should expect this access when hiring a coach, and if the coach thinks otherwise, I suggest moving on to look for someone else.

#5: A great coach will help you avoid getting sidetracked.

Once you've got that nice roadmap with your company's short- and long-term goals in mind, it's still easy to get sidetracked along the way. A coach helps you stay the course, so that you can continue to move toward those goals according to your roadmap. In some cases, a coach may not be there to help you develop your roadmap; they come on the scene once you've got it in place and, in this case, you need someone to help you stay on course. Without those coaches helping me train for my Ironman, I simply would not have been able to compete or finish the race. They kept me from getting sidetracked and losing motivation; they kept me moving forward, making evident progress toward my goal. Good business coaches will continue to help you move toward your

BHAG®, 3HAG, 1 year and other goals outlined in your roadmap. When you can stay focused over the long term and not allow yourself to get distracted by the daily minutiae, you will gain an edge and see results (most likely improved revenue or net profit). As a result, your team will follow and respect you. A great coach can help with all this by keeping you focused on your goals.

#6: A great coach will hold you accountable for outcomes.

If you're the CEO or leader of your business, there's rarely nobody else besides a coach to hold you accountable. In this position, you can tend to get set in your ways, since everyone reports to you. Most of the people in your organization are doers—they'll say yes to you. You will need somebody to push back on you, and to push you to achieve the best results and goals, maximizing the results. Without this accountability, you'll come to accept average results, or results that fall below what you could have achieved. You might turn your company into a lifestyle company that becomes stagnant without a coach holding you accountable. In a lifestyle company, you (and others within your company, taking your lead) just become comfortable: with your current results, current revenue, current salaries, current technology interfaces. If this kind of stagnancy is not corrected, comfort will become the reason the company plateaus over time. The alternative is to be a growth company, which rarely succeeds without a coach. Growth companies are continuing to push their boundaries by taking risks. It's the opposite of being comfortably set in your ways (the lifestyle company). Rather than settling for the status quo with your customers and your quarterly and annual growth ratios, you're actively looking at risks that you could take to expand. You might be looking at additional markets, a new type of product or business model, or thinking of replacing C players with A players. Coaches can help you work through the risks you're looking at and continue to move forward. A good coach will always help you avoid becoming a lifestyle company by holding you accountable for ongoing, measurable progress.

#7: A great coach is an effective sounding-board.

If you have a good coach, you're more likely to have better psychological, mental health. When you have issues as the leader of your company, yet have nobody to turn to and discuss these issues honestly, it will take its toll on you. A good coach will be a good listener who will help you understand what you're going through. They will keep asking you questions. A lot of times, business owners need somebody to listen and understand. You don't necessarily need a coach to come in with all the solutions; you just need a sounding-board to help you make better decisions. It's tough to consistently make the best decisions for your company without a sounding-board that you can be open to and honest with. In my experience, this kind of feedback is essential to your physical health. Stress can produce all kinds of physical problems: ulcers, heart issues, blood issues, and the like. Without that sounding-board in place, it is possible that your physical health will deteriorate over time.

#8: A great coach will provide valuable life and professional experience.

It is important to hire a seasoned business coach so that you can tap into his or her experience and get some real-world feedback about the circumstances you're going through. Perhaps the coach has gone through employee or related issues—whatever their experience may be—you'll be able to tap into that experience for a model to use. This also means that a great coach will share his or her experiences with you, willingly and openly. They won't hold back.

#9: A great coach will focus on team development.

A coach will show an interest in helping you develop and retain top talent for your business. They will involve your leadership team: get them involved in decision-making and make sure your leaders are primed into a senior position so they can eventually take over the business. Employee and leadership-team development is important because, ultimately, you want to be working *on* the business rather than *in* it. You need a good support system in place before you ask, "Who can take this over for me?" If you wait until you're ready to ask that question, you won't have a good answer to your question. A coach should help you look down the road at this need before the need arises. You can work to develop your employees and leaders many ways: sending them to courses, one-on-one coaching, peer-to-peer development, or assign them to work with other leaders in other companies. These are just a few ideas that I've used. Really, the sky's the limit with developing your employees!

#10: A great coach will expose you to fresh ideas in the industry.

If a coach is working in multiple industries, different businesses, and continually educating himself, they are going to bring those ideas back to you and your company. You'll be exposed to new ideas and growing trends within and across your particular industry. Whatever the industry your business is part of, you've got to keep up to date with what's going on and move with the industry rather than stagnate. Kodak is a good example of a business that did not keep up with its industry. They did not anticipate the change or the rate of change toward the digital market with cameras and photo technology. With their blinders on, digital eventually overtook them before they could change with the time. They were outdated overnight, left behind in the paper photo era. A great coach will help your business continue to evolve and develop with changes in technology and industry trends. Without that coach, you won't change as fast, if you do change at all. That slow rate of change could put you out of business altogether in our contemporary, fast-moving business world.

Top 10 Questions for Hiring a Great Coach

Now that you know you need a coach—you understand the value that one can bring to your company—and you know what you're looking for in a coach, you need to look at the essential questions to ask when interviewing coaching candidates. You should plan on having around two or three coaching candidates that you're going to interview. I suggest having ten questions that will help you probe beyond the surface conversations in your interviews of these candidates. It doesn't matter if these coaches are part of a certain coaching group—there are a number of them out there—but each of your candidates should be able

to have big answers to the following questions if
you are going to consider hiring them to coach you.

#1: What is your experience in playing at an elite business level?

In asking this question, you want to make sure
candidates have elite-level experience, because
if they do, you're likely to learn a lot more from
them. If you want to catapult your own company
to that level, you need to know that your coach
has real-world experience at that level. Just like in
competitive sports—whether soccer, rugby, or the
Ironman—you get more respect and insight from
somebody who has played at that level. If they
have, they will know what they're looking for and
how to guide you and your team to get to that level.

#2: What is your average coaching engagement?

It is important to know if a coach's current clients
have seen value from that coach after a period of
time: say, two to six to 18 months. A coach with
a long tenure is more likely to demonstrate the
value he provides to his clients. This question ties
into the coach's ability to bring in new, fresh ideas
to the company. If a coach has a long engagement
with a specific client, it could mean that the coach
has consistently refreshed that business and
brought value to it.

#3: Why do your clients typically leave the coaching relationship with you?

You should ask this question of coaching candidates simply to put them on the spot, to see if they'll be honest. Will they say something like, "I didn't provide the value they were looking for"? Will they object to the question? Will they fake a response? Honesty is an important quality in a coaching relationship.

#4: What does a typical coaching engagement look like?

This question is simply a straightforward request to get him or her to spell out the exact details about when they will meet with you. Monthly? Quarterly? Annually? Something else? Is it a day? A half day? It's important to know what to expect, both for planning your time and your financial investment in hiring a coach. Is the money you're paying worth the frequency or value that he or she is willing to meeting with you?

#5: What are some personal successes you've had in business?

If one coach can tell you he has grown companies by five percent, yet a different one can tell you they've done twenty to thirty percent year-over-year, then I'd be more likely to go with the higher-growth coach. This question probes for some impressive success stories in business.

#6: What do you do to "sharpen the saw"?

It's important to understand what a coach does personally to keep that razor-sharp edge on new approaches, new techniques, and evolving industry trends. How do they stay current, relevant, and fresh? If the coach stumbles to answer this question, they may not be placing enough emphasis on their own professional development and networking.

#7: What is your network like and how will those connections help me?

When you hire a coach, you are—to a degree—buying that coach's network. This network has the potential to provide you with extensive expertise across your industry and other industries that neither you nor your coach can provide. It also broadens your opportunities for growth, both within and outside of your current market. Such networking may also inject additional investment opportunities into your business. If a coach balks at this question, take note. They may not be willing to extend their network to you.

#8: If you were sitting here one year from now, what would success in my company look like to you?

First, this question assumes that you've previously gone into some detail as to your business, its model, its vision, its roadmap, and its current employee, fiscal, and leadership status. For your coaching candidate to accurately respond to this question, they need to have some context for understanding your business and its many components.

Second, you want to put them on the spot with this question and see if his goals for both the business and for yourself match, exceed, or fall below what you're looking for. Obviously, if their goals fall below what you're looking for, you'll likely drop that candidate from the list. If their goals far exceed yours, I tend to see that as a good thing. It's evidence that they can bring fresh perspectives and understanding to the business and can hold you accountable to the goals you've currently set while pushing you to think outside of your expectations. If their goals are higher than yours, there's potential that they could help you exceed even your goals and get to a higher level you didn't even think existed.

#9: What other experts would you recommend or bring on board?

This question could shed light on a coach's weaknesses, including how they would go about compensating for them. For example, if you've got a coaching candidate who has a lot of operational experience, but one of your company's goals is growth and sales, he or she might suggest bringing on a sales expert as well. Or maybe there's an issue in your business with retention and high turnover. Will this coach suggest bringing in some type of an HR people-expert to help fill in those areas of weakness? This question also demonstrates that we cannot assume any one coach will help in all the areas you need. Like with my Ironman, you may need more than one coach.

#10: Why would I hire you compared to other coaches I'm talking to?

In asking this question, you simply want the candidate to summarize their overall value as a coach both to the business and to yourself. In one last summary, why are they a good fit for you? It's the elevator pitch: brief and to the point.

Conclusion

I particularly remember an external CFO coming into our company between 2007 and 2008 to conduct numerous evaluations. As a result, he recommended to our leadership team that we stop offering construction services because we were losing money and it was severely affecting our cash flow. As a result of this advice, we stopped bidding construction jobs and shut down that division. We acted on this just before the markets crashed later that year, causing thousands of construction companies to go out of business. That particular coach's advice saved our business from a failure that could have destroyed everything we had built.

It's important to be able to easily identify the qualities of great coaches, and it can be tricky to vet and hire an effective coach for your business. The methods for selecting a coach and characteristics of great coaches I've shared in this chapter will help you navigate the process and make a wise, productive selection. I hope you'll put these methods into practice so that you can make progress on executing your roadmap and eventually cross the finish line of all the goals you've set. Just remember, coaches are vital partners to helping each of us—athletes, spouses, parents, investors, employees, and business leaders—achieve our goals and cross the finish line!

Chapter 8

Facing Adversity, Hitting the Wall, and Pushing Through

Before I decided to train for my first Ironman, I had started off playing soccer and then rugby. That was about it. I also began to run a little, although I had never engaged formal training for running. It dawned on me to begin the Ironman path once I started hitting personal bests along the way: three, then four, then five miles. After that, I was then persuaded to run a half marathon. A few weeks after completing my half marathon, I began to think about smaller triathlons and then eventually an Ironman. It's the same with all the disciplines within an Ironman race. You start off with small goals and work your way up, proving to yourself all along the way that you can do more. Once you start beating those personal bests, breaking through those personal barriers, you start to think you're invincible. You might begin to wonder what other crazy events—such as Ultras or extreme challenges—are out there to compete in. In short, your thinking processes change about who you are, what you're capable of, and what you want to tackle. Whether in sports or business, engaging and overcoming such obstacles is mostly a mind game.

Breaking through Mental Barriers

For example, one time I was out on a bike ride and within about 15 miles of leaving the house, I had already had three flat tires! It became super frustrating to me as I went along. Normally, you might get one flat tire every three weeks when you're training competitively. I had three in one ride within 20 miles! So, all these thoughts began to go through my head. (That's typical when you begin to face adversity; the thoughts start to creep in.) I was in the middle of nowhere, and began wondering, "Do I just go home? Do I just try and call my neighbor or something?" At these crucial times, when you begin to start questioning yourself, it always goes back to discipline. Will you stick to your training schedule, even with all the difficulty? In this case, I decided, "No—I won't quit. I need to get this done. I've allocated this amount of time to do this ride." So, I ended up finding out where the nearest bike shop was and managed to lug through and get there. I was two or three miles away, riding on flat tires—not fun! I bought the supplies I needed and continued my 100-mile ride that day. The whole ride took an hour or so longer than it should have, but I felt a sense of accomplishment at the end of that day, upon returning home. It was a super-powerful experience for me and again helped build that mental strength needed to break through the barriers. Without this kind of mental training, I might not have finished the Ironman.

Another example of breaking through mental barriers, which I mention early in this book, is bike training in group rides. In the beginning, I'd typically be left behind, or be at the very back of the pack. I'd return home from these rides totally exhausted: come in the door and just collapse. But I persisted. I kept going out riding with that group, probably two or three times a week. As I continued, I became more aware of the group's changes in speed and could anticipate how to stay with them. Not only that, but I was becoming physically conditioned to keep pace. Eventually, by mentally not giving up in the beginning, I was able to break through my physical limitations and occasionally lead the group from the front.

Competitive Spirit

I have a natural competitive spirit. That, coupled with my own stubbornness, allowed me to persist where some others may have given up. In business, you need that same competitive spirit and stubbornness: the drive to continue no matter what. Otherwise, you could be sidetracked before you even begin to really implement your roadmap. You have to stubbornly pursue that vision for your company. When you persist, incremental breakthroughs will happen, just as they did for my Ironman training. First, beating my personal bests eventually inspired me to sign on for the Sprint, Olympic, and half Ironman distance races before reaching for the stretch goal of a full Ironman. Later, while training, my persistence in spite of failure and various mental barriers to progress produced breakthroughs that continued to inspire me to continue training, which produced increased breakthroughs all along the way! I just knew I wasn't going to give up or allow minor issues to get in my way. This tenacity is required of serious athletes and serious business leaders.

Race Day

After all the training, the Ironman race day finally arrived. I had been through all kinds of training: physical, mental, nutritional, skills-related—you name it. I was ready. I managed to just get through the swim, having been beaten up: punched in the face and kicked in the head and body. Unexpectedly, the swim was a pretty bruising event for me to complete. But I finished it, and then decided I was going to have fun! So, I got on the bike, which was amazing! I paced myself well, there was a little bit of wind, and I was getting the necessary nutrition. I thought everything was going well with my nutrition and, after five and a half hours, I completed the bike portion. By this time in the race, I was thinking, "Yeah, great. I'm a runner! I liked the training and I pitched my long runs out there." About 15 miles into the running part of the Ironman—which was about two hours into the run—I really started to struggle. I was struggling to find the energy to continue—I hit that wall hard. My mental roll began to play all the negative thinking, and a lot of people I had passed earlier in the race were now passing me. One of my training partners had been running alongside me in the race. In training, I was normally able to stay a little bit ahead of her, but in the race, at this point, I had to stop—I just couldn't go any more. I had no energy left. So, I worked through the mental barriers, the questions: "Do I quit? Do I keep going?" I resolved that, "No! I'm not going to let people down. I've got this vision ahead of me and I'm not going to give up." From that point forward in the race, I had to make my mind up again to press forward. I took it step by step: in small incremental steps, measuring my progress between each station. Food and drink at each station allowed me to walk through that few hundred yards before beginning to run again. I measured my progress as I ran the next mile or two between each aid station. After about six miles of this, I began to feel refreshed. I could pace again and was able to start running hard! In the last half mile, I sprinted to the finish line and crossed it with a sense of exhilaration and accomplishment that I could not compare to any previous experience!

Hitting that wall is also an inevitable part of leading businesses. If you know it's coming, it's wise to prepare your response to it ahead of time. You'll be that much tougher mentally if your mind can already be made up beforehand. When you get there, you'll have to go through an evaluation of where you stand. You look at all the people you've talked to about the race: family, friends, clients, the people that have come to support you. They're all watching you, so you don't want to let them down. (In my Ironman race, I was also inspired by the grit and determination of some who were racing in spite of physical disabilities.) Again, you set your goals early and get that vision out in front of you, and remind yourself of them often! Whether you're in a race or in a business, the ability to mentally step back and evaluate where you are is invaluable to your progress and success.

Facing Adverse Circumstances

On one of my early morning bike training rides someone out in front had fallen so that it caused a bunch of cyclists to crash as well. (It had been raining the night before so the roads were extra slippery.) I ended up falling off my bike in this wreck as well and was pretty scraped up. Worst of all, I had badly damaged my shoulder. While it wasn't a dislocation, it was a serious shoulder injury and was pretty painful. I began to think, "I'm only eight to 10 weeks out from the race. All this training that I've done is just finished. There's no way I'm going to be able to compete!" I was definitely depressed for two or three days. After that, the swelling began to subside and I began to reevaluate my circumstances. There was no break and no dislocation. So, I began to talk to my experts and coaches, and they did an evaluation of how bad my injury was. I started some treatment on my shoulder. Also, I think my determination, fueled by my vision to compete in the Ironman, went a long way in the mental struggle related to my injury. I kept thinking of not wanting to let everyone down who had supported me while I had been training. So I started to train around my injury. I was able to start a degree of biking again, and eased back into a lot of running. Eventually, I realized I could focus on all my other strength areas and not give up training those areas just because of my shoulder.

Some people may have used this kind of injury as an excuse to quit. They would have called off the race and stopped training altogether. These are the times, in Ironman races, in business, and in life, when you have to know how to dig deep and see what's in your character that will enable you to persist against the odds. It's called grit— determination. Use those experts—coaches and others who have the professional backgrounds you need strength in—to train you in your and your company's strengths in spite of the weaknesses or injuries.

Every business will face adversity, mental challenges, and hit a wall. I've found that the key to successfully navigating such times is to take a step back, remove yourself from the swirl of thoughts and negative mental talk, and evaluate where you are from an unemotional, objective position. (That coach you've hired should be helpful to you here.) Get with your leadership team and strategize how you will move forward in spite of the setbacks or difficulties. As needed, modify your course, your roadmap, your training plan, or your plan of action. No matter how airtight your roadmap, and no matter how clearly communicated your goals, methods, expectations, and culture, things still go wrong in business along the way. The unexpected always arrives on the scene, eventually. Take that step back, evaluate, and give yourself permission to look at workarounds, or different methods for achieving the same objectives. Perhaps set aside the issue altogether for a time and focus on other areas that require your help at that time where you can still progress in your roadmap.

Just remember, in whatever aspect of living you find passion, challenge, and that competitive spirit of grit and determination arising in your heart, the Ironman is not an Ironman because he or she can do things with ease while perfectly meeting all expectations. He or she's an Ironman because they refuse to give up and insists on crossing the finish line, no matter what.

Enjoyed this book?

For further information please visit my website at
www.theradixgroupllc.com or contact me directly.

Robert Clinkenbeard co-founded one of the largest landscape companies (ILM) in the South West Region of the United States back in 2001. The company grew to 350+ employees with 5 branches and revenue more than $20M. The company had a very successful exit back in 2016.

Since Robert has had the experience to scale a company up quickly, he is now focused on coaching other CEO's and Key Executives in business and personal growth. He is currently becoming certified with Gazelles/Scaling Up Coaching organization and Gravitas Impact Premium Coaches and is closely working with various peer and mastermind groups.

Robert is the past President of the AZ Chapter of the Entrepreneur's Organization (EO) and has helped grow the EO Accelerator program globally to 9 regions. He also currently serves on the EO Western Regional Council's Board as an Area Director. In December 2017 he completed his two-year term as the President of the Arizona Landscape Contractors Association.

Robert was raised in Edinburgh, Scotland and moved to Arizona in 1999 to find a better lifestyle, new opportunities, and to widen his traveling options. He has travelled to nearly 30 countries and his goal is to visit 50 countries including Nepal, Argentina and Iceland. Robert now lives in South Carolina and has been married for eight years to his wife, Faith, and is kept busy with five children. He played competitive rugby and soccer for 20 years and has competed in 4 Ironman triathlon events, so he fully understands discipline, strategy and execution.

Robert Clinkenbeard
Owner – The Radix Group LLC
CEO/Global Business Coach
Mobile/Office: 480-251-2366
robert@theradixgroupllc.com
www.theradixgroupllc.com